Sharing Hope, Nurturing Resilience

A Coaching Journey

Dee Fowler Anderson

Disclaimer

The content of this book is for general instruction only. Each person's physical, emotional, and spiritual condition is unique. The instruction in this book is not intended to replace or interrupt the reader's relationship with a physician or other professional. Please consult your doctor for matters pertaining to your specific health and diet.

Author Photograph: Craig S. Nelson
Cover Design and Interior Layout: Bethany Snyder

To contact the publisher, visit: www.resilientyoucoaching.com
To contact the author, visit: www.resilientyoucoaching.com

ISBN-13: 978-1511664103
ISBN-10: 151166410X

Printed in the United States of America

Contents

Introduction

"Your life has purpose. Your story is important. Your dreams count. Your voice matters. You were born to make an impact."

I remember sharing with a friend, when our children were very small, that I didn't think I could survive if anything ever happened to one of my children. Many years later, I would find that I would be tested—or so it seemed. I never thought I would experience someone I love living with a serious mental illness. And then I received a call that my oldest son had been arrested. My world fell apart. I couldn't believe this was my life. In the confusing days that followed, I realized my son did not have a grip on reality, or understand the seriousness of the charges against him. Something was clearly wrong. It hit me like a ton of bricks: My son had a serious mental illness.

I didn't have a clue how to walk this road; I was on a journey without a map. In the last several years, I have learned to negotiate uncharted, scary territories—the judicial, probation, and medical/psychiatric systems. Most profoundly, I have discovered the importance of self-care in the face of sometimes unbearable stress.

I never imagined that one day I would see this whole experience as a gift. Today, I know that it was all a part of my healing journey, and that I have been coached along the way into my life's purpose. Each new roller coaster ride that I encountered made me more aware of stress and how it manifested in my body. I discovered tools along the way that helped me mitigate the toll that stress can have on one's body.

Sharing Hope, Nurturing Resilience: A Coaching Journey is for parents who live courageously every day with children with disabilities. It is for students seeking a support system that will help them mitigate the stresses of being away from home and on their own for the first time. This book is for those who want to model being resilient individuals in the face of whatever life throws at them.

My journey has taken me from licensed Occupational Therapist to a resilient Health Coach. This is how I think of myself now. I continue to develop and grow in personal resilience and the ability to encourage others in discovering their own resilience. When people ask me what I do, I respond, "I am a Health Coach." Most people are familiar with the term "coach" in relationship to a sports team, but I think of it as helping individuals discover their own "hidden wholeness."

As each new challenge was set before me in learning to care for my son, and to take care of myself in the process, I was encouraged to "keep on walking." I discovered that I had the tools and skills to make this journey after all. And when I was lacking something, the right person or opportunity would come along to guide me. With each halting step, I learned to trust myself and the process. I discovered my own personal gifts, which include curiosity, deep listening, and encouragement. Now I am determined to use these gifts to help others become their best, resilient self.

On this journey, I have had to learn to cope with grief, guilt, shame, stigma and isolation—all are terribly painful and intensely stressful. To be honest, I was angry at first, looking for someone to blame for this unfair new reality. I came to understand that I was grieving the loss of the son I had known and the life I had anticipated for him. Guilt would overtake me at times, when I wondered if there was something I could have done differently to prevent this from happening to my son. Many still see mental illness as a character flaw or the result of family dysfunction, rather than the biological brain disorder that it is. This only serves to reinforce stigma, isolation, and pain. My education as an Occupational Therapist helped me to understand this on an intellectual level, but my heart needed to catch up. This was happening to my son and my family.

As an Occupational Therapist, I was trained to treat the whole person—occupational, emotional, social, intellectual, financial, physical, and spiritual. Now I needed to apply this to myself, to develop self-trust and develop strategies that would help me be a resilient caregiver for my son, and to allow myself to continue to live fully with and for the rest of my family. Chronic, repetitive stress can have devastating consequences for one's health.

My challenges included finding information and support, as well as being reminded of the importance of self-care. I found these needs met when I discovered the National Alliance on Mental Illness (NAMI) and joined a local chapter. The Family to Family 12 week course was exactly what I as a parent needed on this frightening and seemingly hopeless journey. I needed accurate information, support, and a safe place to share my heartbreaking story with others who "got it." I was also encouraged to be vigilant about my own self-care. Being connected to others was and continues to be so important on this journey. My support from NAMI helped so much to relieve the effects of loneliness, isolation, and stigma.

During this same time, with encouragement from members from my spiritual community, I took the risk to be part of a coaching for transformation team. While it was something new to me, it seemed to be the right amount of "stress" to engage me intellectually, and served to build my resilience. As part of my training, I received six months of individual coaching sessions from a fabulous coach from the Auburn Coaching Institute. What fortuitous timing to have a coach walking alongside me during this time of my life's journey. I also began to perceive the "Spirit" as my ever-present "coach." I experienced this as an organic process, where the "Spirit" came along side me, helping me to clarify and encouraging me to take necessary next right steps on this journey.

It was through the Auburn Coaching Institute that I was first introduced to the Wheel of Life. The various sections of the wheel represent different aspects of a person, and the whole wheel represents balance. We were encouraged to rate our level of satisfaction in each area, and determine where we needed to find more balance. I used this to guide me in balancing my life with more physical activity, making changes in my physical environment, eating healthier, developing new spiritual practices, and connecting with others.

With the guidance of my coaches, I did not get stuck in the anger or paralyzing questions of "Why my family?" After all, why would I think my family would be immune to this devastating illness and its resulting stress. According to statistics, mental illness strikes one in five people at some point in their lives. I decided to make the changes that would help me to survive—and maybe even thrive—amidst the chaos. While everyone is different in their response to stress and in what helps them to overcome it, I have decided to share my experience and walk along with others as they take steps on their own personal journey to wholeness.

This book is meant to be an extension to my coaching skills. Each of us knows deep in our soul what we need to be healthy, and my desire is that you begin to trust that inner voice, the "Spirit," what Lissa Rankin calls your "inner pilot light." Along the way, let's share hope and nurture wholeness in one another. Trust the journey. My hope is for you to survive whatever life throws your way. Better yet: thrive!

Chapter 1:
Understand Yourself

"Knowing yourself is the beginning of all wisdom." —Aristotle

Cesar Milan says, "We don't get the dog we want, we get the dog we need." He feels the dog a person chooses comes into their life and teaches them the lessons they need most. Two years ago, my husband wanted to get a dog to replace our previous family pet. I wasn't so sure this was a good idea. Our children were grown and out of the house. I wanted to be free to travel and not worry about who was going to take care of the dog. He started looking, though, and showed me some little French Brittany Spaniels in North Carolina. They were cute, but I was still holding out.

The breeder uses the French naming system, and all dogs born that particular year had names starting with letter H. Hope stole my heart right from the beginning. The breeder wanted to talk with us, learn our personalities, and try to match the "right" pup with its new owners. Lord knows, I needed hope! Long story short, we were able to bring Hope home—literally and figuratively.

Hope is always present, very intently aware of what is going on around her. She is in tune with the energy that exudes from each person, whether it is strong or fragile. Somehow, when we set the intention of how we want her to behave, she seems to "get it." I believe she feels that energy and responds appropriately. She always greets my elderly, frail parents in a gentle and calm way. Now, mind you, she is a otherwise exuberant two-year-old pup! When we share Hope with my parents, it is obvious that she is a sweet, gentle balm for their souls. They smile more and, yes, even look more hopeful. So there you have it! Hope is my teacher. In this case, I got the dog I wanted and the dog I needed. She teaches me presence, trust, confidence, and awareness. She continues to teach me to share hope, and for that I am grateful.

I am grateful, too, for other lessons in how to share hope. My friend and favorite musician/storyteller, david m. bailey, flamed hope in the hearts of thousands by going on the road and sharing his story of survival. On July 4, 1996, doctors told david he had a malignant brain tumor and would be dead by Christmas. david left his corporate job and returned to his first love of songwriting and singing, with a goal of sharing the hope on which his life depended.

I first experienced david's ministry of music at a transformation conference in North Carolina. I was touched by his message and the way he shared his story of survival with such humility and authenticity. One song he shared, "Her Favorite Color Was Green," was about a girl he knew who died too young. The song moved through the anger and confusion of such a time to a real sense of hope. It affected me profoundly, as my family, along with many others in the community, had recently experienced the tragic loss of three young friends.

The following year, when I saw my then 17-year-old son and his friends weeping at the one-year anniversary of the accident, I became convinced that david needed to come and share his message of hope. We began to talk about a plan. I had no experience in planning such an event. I had no idea how I would fund such an undertaking. david said, "Let's keep talking. We will make this happen." And we did. Memories of how the three boys lived with great passion on and off the soccer field highlighted david's challenge and inspiration for all listeners to treasure the beauty of each new day, and to live life with that same kind of passion. I like to believe that we created a sacred space where healing could begin.

My friendship and collaboration with david was an important part of my beginning to understand my purpose. It was also an important part of my healing journey. david succumbed to the ravages of glioblastoma in 2010. david surely was, and continues through his music to be, a reflection of light and hope for many—me included. And I am grateful.

It always astonishes me to discover how connected we are, and how we are all on a journey individually, but also collectively. Life is a journey, a journey of discovering our purpose and, in the process, uncovering and shaping our values. On this journey, we will inevitably face challenges and encounter stress.

Stress is a normal part of life. Things that happen to you or around you, and things that you do or think, put stress on your body. You can experience stress from your environment, your body, and your thoughts. Stress is the body's reaction to change that requires an adjustment or response.

It's amazing when you think about it: The body is miraculously made to experience stress and react to it. A just-right amount of stress can be positive, a motivator. In this instance, stress supports achievement of a particular goal, and is experienced as exhilarating. The stress hormone cortisol then returns to a normal level. Stress alerts us to danger, and prepares us for either flight or fight. But stress can be negative when one experiences continuous, repetitive challenges without relief, or without experiencing the opposing relaxation response between challenges. Ironically, that same mechanism that protects us from danger may also sabotage our bodies and minds. Both kinds of stress release cortisol as part of the body's adaptive response. Once that alarm has been sounded and the stress hormone is released, there has to be a relaxation response to counter it.

In our present fast-paced lives, individuals are constantly

bombarded with stress. This is just everyday stress, and doesn't include major stressful life events. So many of us live in a compromised state, with high cortisol levels keeping us in a perpetual state of heightened alert. This is a major problem, and can have devastating consequences for our health.

Stress symptoms can affect your body, thoughts, and feelings, as well as your behavior. Stress that is left unmitigated can contribute to health problems such as high blood pressure, heart disease, obesity, and diabetes. In fact, I believe it weakens our immune system and leaves us susceptible to many diseases. Stress can literally kill you!

The first step in managing stress is to be aware of stress symptoms and how they feel in your body, because everyone is different. Common effects of stress on the body include headache, muscle tension or pain, chest pain, fatigue, stomach upset, sleep problems, and a change in sex drive. Mood changes include anxiety, restlessness, lack of motivation or focus, irritability or anger, sadness, and depression. Stress can also alter behavior and manifest in over- or under-eating, drug or alcohol abuse, tobacco use, and social withdrawal. The key is learning to listen to your body, and knowing when you are experiencing too much stress without relief.

Now, here is a funny story. I've been feeling a little stressed for a couple of days. I woke up this morning to discover my laptop had stopped working, we are in the middle of a major snowstorm, and my dog is sick. Things are a little stressful at work, too; staff has been affected by a death in the family and health issues. It's also compounded by my coursework at IIN®, and by my book-writing schedule.

I'm feeling the stress as tension and tightness in my neck and shoulders, fatigue, lack of focus, and eating foods I don't normally crave or eat. And then there is the breathing—or lack thereof. I always notice that when I'm stressed, I do a lot of sighing, and my breathing is tight and shallow. I'm writing a book about stress and how to manage it, and today I'm experiencing all these stressors! I'm like, "Enough already. I get it! I don't need any more lessons in order to share with others!" Maybe I just needed to experience how stress feels again, so I can get real with my description. Although I think I could do it without the additional lesson, thank you.

As for my response to the stress? I'm still learning. Apparently, it's a life-long journey! When I told this story to a chat partner, she said, "I hope it is the last one." I responded, "Oh, it won't be, and I know that. Stress is a normal part of life. I know it's all about how we respond with our own wisdom."

The Whole Self

Understanding yourself depends on your awareness of all the aspects of the self. One model that depicts this visually is the Wheel of Life. It encompasses the Spiritual, Emotional, Social, Occupational, Physical, Intellectual, and Financial aspects of the self. Health and resilience occurs when these aspects are relatively in balance.

Ironically, my search for wholeness began with my

acknowledgement of my brokenness. I needed to show hospitality to myself, to give myself what I needed most: a tincture of time to be whole and healthy. This journey to health is both messy and beautiful, both excruciating and beautiful. It is not unlike the birthing process. It is hard work, messy, painful—and at the same time, beautiful.

Barbara Bloom says, "When the Japanese mend broken objects they aggrandize the damage by filling the cracks with gold, because they believe that when something's suffered damage and has a history it becomes more beautiful." What I want you to understand is that it is okay to be broken. It is okay to take your time. It is okay! Brokenness, like stress, will happen over and over again because life is a journey, and when we embark on the journey, we will encounter both. It is not a straight line, but more like a spiral. We keep revisiting what we need to learn to be our authentic self. Each time we rebirth a new, more whole self.

This Advent season, I am keenly aware of the waiting and the birthing of another, more whole, healthy, and resilient me. Every aspect of me is growing as I journey to become a resilient Health Coach and author. I hope it is beautiful also in the sense that it helps you to discover and uniquely develop a more resilient you.

Where do you experience brokenness? Acknowledge it. Name it. Where do you sense something wanting to be born in you? Give it time. Nurture it. Because chances are, the world needs it. And it needs your unique self to deliver it.

The Spiritual Self

The spiritual self may be defined differently by each individual, but at its core, spirituality helps by giving us a foundation from which to live. It is not necessarily connected to a belief system or religious worship. It comes from understanding your connection to yourself and others, your values, and your search for a meaningful life. For many, the spiritual self is expressed in religious observance, prayer, meditation, or a belief in a higher power. Others feel connected and supported spiritually in nature, music, art, or a secular community.

When I revisited the Wheel of Life during coach training, I pondered deeply how it reflected me as a whole person. I discovered that my faith is the center of "who I am." I adapted the wheel to reflect that, because I believe we are all spiritual beings in a material world. Rather than being a slice of the pie, I see spirituality as the framework or spokes of the wheel. This is true for me because all the aspects of me—emotional, social, intellectual, physical, occupational, and financial—are informed by my faith.

While I will share some ways I remain spiritually balanced, please remember that the Spiritual Self is your unique way of being in the world. It is how you understand yourself, relate to others, and interact with all of creation. It's about acting in alignment with your values and living out your purpose, a meaningful life.

A simple spiritual tool for letting go is a prayer box. It is best to have an actual, physical container with a lid. Mine is a carved wooden box. The process begins with writing a note with the name of the person about whom you are concerned or stressed, or a description of the situation that you so obsessively want to fix. Place it in the box. Close the lid. Let it go. It really is as simple as that. You may also say a prayer or imagine the person or situation surrounded by light and air, both of which are healing.

The willingness to do this comes from realizing there are many things in life that you cannot control, heal, or fix. Sometimes it is just best to let it go. When you do that, sometimes you will find yourself "coached" into a next right step to take on the journey. This reflection, a spiritual inquisitiveness, is a pathway through the mind that transforms the heart. It may shift your thoughts only a fraction of a degree, but it is enough to change everything in that moment.

For me to remain spiritually balanced, each morning as I make my bed I reflect on the lyrical words of wisdom imprinted on a canvas above my bed. They are a reminder from my friend david bailey that life is fleeting, that we have a limited time to make a difference in the world and to share hope with others. It becomes my morning prayer that I will pay attention and have the courage to "be the difference" on this particular day.

As you can see, it does not have to be an elaborate process. It can be a simple ritual and a powerful reminder. Are you satisfied with your spiritual wellness?

- Do you make time for meditation and/or prayer?

- Do your values guide your decisions and actions?

- Are you accepting of the views of others?

If you are not happy with your spiritual wellness, what steps will you take to become more balanced?

The Emotional Self

The emotional self is very complex and has implications for all other aspects of the self. Emotional wellness helps you connect socially by maintaining satisfying relationships based on mutual commitment, trust, and respect. The emotional self helps in the intellectual dimension to make personal choices and decisions based on the integration of feelings, thoughts, philosophies, and behavior. It also works with the occupational self to manage your life in personally rewarding ways, and working independently while realizing the importance of seeking and appreciating the support and assistance of others. While emotional health does imply an ability to cope with stress effectively, it is more than that. It is also our awareness of and acceptance of our feelings (rather than denial of them), having an optimistic approach to life, and enjoying life despite its occasional disappointments and frustrations.

Do you feel balanced in your emotional dimension?

- Are you able to maintain a balance of work, family, friends, and other obligations?

- Do you have ways to reduce stress in your life?

- Are you able to make decisions with a minimum of stress and worry?

If you are not satisfied with your emotional wellness, what steps will you take to become more balanced?

The Social Self

Who are you socially? Are you the one who thinks out loud while you talk? Are you the quiet one who takes time to slowly process situations? Are you energized by being with people? Do you need time alone to regenerate? It is important to identify and acknowledge the authentic you. This will help you make choices to enhance personal relationships, maintain valuable friendships, and contribute to your living environment and community.

Personally, I identify socially as introverted. I tend to be very sensitive to social and sensory stimulation. It was with great interest that I read *Quiet: The Power of Introverts in a World That Can't Stop Talking* by Susan Cain. She describes introverts processing information, both physical and emotional, from their environments unusually deeply, which can be exhausting. While I enjoy fellowship and being connected to family and friends, I also know when I have had enough and need to retreat to rejuvenate. In this way, I honor who I am and the wisdom I possess to care for my social self.

Another aspect of social wellness emphasizes contributing to the well-being of our environment and others around us. I believe it is a reminder of our purpose or reason for being. I have experienced brokenness and loss. I have also learned to survive—indeed, thrive. How did this happen? I was surrounded by family and friends who responded to my urgent texts for prayers and held me when I wept. While they did not try to fix anything for me, they sat with me and listened deeply. With this enveloping love and the tincture of time, my pain evolved into a desire to help others through workshops, coaching, and writing this book.

Do you feel balanced in your social dimension?

- Do you plan time to be with your family and friends?

- Are your relationships with others positive and rewarding?

- Do you explore diversity by interacting with people of other cultures, backgrounds, and beliefs?

If you are not satisfied with your social wellness, what steps will you take to become more balanced?

The Physical Self

The physical dimension encompasses the need for regular physical activity. First, consider your body type and what kind of exercise you need: strengthening, flexibility, and/or endurance. Listen to your body. What do you need to feel balanced? It makes sense to choose a physical activity that you enjoy. My most sustainable exercise routines have their roots in my childhood pastimes. I thoroughly enjoy exercising with a weighted hula hoop, and the rhythmical movements of Tai Chi remind me of my love of dancing. Daily walking in the fresh air and sunshine is a simple way to keep active.

In addition, I feel balanced when I get plenty of sleep each night and eat a balanced diet of fresh fruits and vegetables, clean protein, cheese, nuts, seeds, and a small amount of grains. It is important for you to experiment with different ways of eating, and, most importantly, listen to your body in how it responds to different foods. Different people need different types of nutrition to stay healthy, and your food requirements will likely change over time. In general, you will feel healthier by increasing fruits and vegetables, decreasing sugar and processed foods, and drinking more water. I have always felt that our physical body is a gift to us to use while we are on this earth, and it is our responsibility to care for it as best we can.

Do you feel balanced in your physical dimension?

- Do you get a sufficient amount of sleep?
- Do you have an established exercise routine?
- Do you eat a nutritionally balanced diet?

If you are not satisfied with your physical wellness, what steps will you take to become more balanced?

The Intellectual Self

The intellectual dimension recognizes your creative, challenging mental activities. In your search for intellectual health, you will expand your knowledge and skills while discovering opportunities for sharing your gifts with others. For me, coaching skills training helped me to discover and expand my skills of deep listening, encouragement, and curiosity. It also challenged me to develop and learn new skills and seek out new resources for growth.

I have been blessed with colleagues, friends, and family who have encouraged me in my writing and challenged me in learning about new cultures and ideas. The positive messages surrounding me have helped me to see new possibilities for my creative self. I have been stretched in numerous beneficial ways. Yes, I have felt vulnerable and more than a little afraid, but I continue to gain so much clarity and direction. I am grateful for all of it.

Do you feel balanced in your intellectual dimension?

- Are you open to new ideas?
- Do you seek personal growth by learning new skills?
- Do you look for ways to use creativity?

If you are not satisfied with your intellectual wellness, what steps will you take to become more balanced?

The Occupational Self

Through my training as an occupational therapist, I understand the occupational self is much more than relationship to a job or career. It is about how we spend our time and energy on things that are meaningful to us as individuals. This has such a strong link to our spiritual self. It is worth remembering that the spiritual self is your unique way of being in the world. It is how you understand yourself, relate to others, and interact with all of creation. It's about aligning your values and living out your purpose. Of course, you have to work on determining your values. Mine happen to be my faith as the center of my life; being open to suggestions and growth; enjoying time with family and friends; having my work support my family; honoring and caring for my body, mind, and soul; and valuing integrity (walking the talk). These all help to determine how I will use my time and energy in the occupational dimension of myself. My goal is to fulfill my purpose of nurturing health and resilience in you and others in some small way. I know I feel most balanced when my life and purpose fit authentically together.

Do you feel balanced in your occupational dimension?

- Do you enjoy going to work each day? Or do you engage in other meaningful activities throughout your day?

- Do you have a manageable work load or activity schedule?

- Are you able to talk to your boss, co-workers, or fellow participants when problems arise?

If you are not satisfied with your occupational wellness, what steps will you take to become more balanced?

The Financial Self

The financial dimension recognizes that our attitude toward and relationship with money have a significant effect on our overall health. If there is any one thing that will bring peace and contentment into the human heart, and into the family, it is to live within our means. And if there is any one thing that is grinding and discouraging and disheartening, it is to have debts and obligations that we cannot meet. Proper money management and living within your means are essential in today's world, if we are to live abundantly and happily. As you travel the wellness path, you'll learn to manage money before it manages you, use self-discipline and self-restraint in money matters, and develop a budget to get out of debt. The financial dimension of wellness entails realizing it is not the amount of money an individual earns that brings peace of mind; it is developing a discipline of saving to prepare for short-term, long-term, and emergency expenses, and responsibly managing resources.

Financially, I strive to have enough money to live the life that makes my heart sing, which really comes down to following my passions and fulfilling my purpose. I try to focus on the things that matter most to me, and on the things that I can control. I was able to work as a licensed Occupational Therapist for several years. During that time, I was able to contribute financially to my family and move forward in my journey to nurture wholeness in the students with whom I worked. At the same time, I was able to participate in Coaching Skills training. For the last few years, I have worked as a coordinator for the literacy piece of our community health improvement project. Again, it has allowed me to contribute to my family, work in the area of my passion and purpose, and has helped me finance my further Health Coach training at IIN and write this book. Now, I don't intend to imply that this path has been clear and straight. It has helped to have a financial plan, to live within our means while I work toward fulfilling my purpose.

Do you feel balanced in your financial dimension?

- Do you have a budget and track your monthly expenses?
- Do you spend less than 25% on your mortgage or rent?
- Do you have an emergency fund to cover at least three months of living expenses?

If you are not satisfied with your financial wellness, what steps will you take to become more balanced?

Now, you and I both know that none of us is ever completely balanced in all the dimensions of the whole self. Life is often messy, uncertain, and unpredictable. You do the best you can. Someone once said, "The key to balance is to know when you've lost it." How true. Then you can respond with your inner wisdom to restore it, or at least inch a little closer to having all the parts working together. As my friend and mentor david bailey advised, "Let your life be an art." Piece it together in such a way that your life matters. It is not about the largeness or celebrity of your life, but the quality, the way it impacts those around you, one person at a time.

Chapter 2:
Fulfill Your Purpose

"Your purpose in life is to find your purpose and give your
whole heart and soul to it." —Gautama Buddha

When I tell people that I am a coach, I know they envision a
sports team coach or athletic trainer. I suppose in the best sense
of the word, the two are similar. My youngest son had a soccer
coach whose philosophy was that he did all he could during
practices to develop ball skills, game strategies, and condition-
ing for his players. When it was game time, he said, "My work
is done, and the players, individually and as a team, have to
execute what they have learned." He was then an encourager on
the sidelines. Similarly, as a Health Coach, my role is to listen
deeply to my clients, encourage them to make the changes they
identify to be healthier, ask questions to help them gain clarity

about their purpose, and help them align their own purpose and passion. They have to make the choices and put their insights and intents into action.

I intuitively know I am here for a greater purpose. Each of us has been given gifts that lead us in a certain direction. We all have incredible potential within us just waiting to be tapped. Like a tiny acorn that has everything inside it to become a mighty oak, you have everything inside you to become who you are meant to be. Knowing who you are and what you can become will help you clarify your purpose. It is hard work. It is heart work. You must accept personal responsibility for discovering your own unique gifts, and intentionally put them to purposeful use. My gifts are deep listening, curiosity, and encouragement, and I know my purpose is to coach others to be more resilient in the face of whatever life brings them.

In this journey of life it is important that we develop our ability to become navigators—that is, to become resilient individuals. Paying attention to the trail markers, equipping ourselves, and harnessing these resources to keep on walking make all the difference. In many cases, we simply make the best of what resources we have available at the time. And we look for the means and methods to improve our resources.

So I began taking coaching for transformation skill training. In this training, I attained knowledge that would help me walk this strange, new road of caring for my grown son with a serious mental illness. I saw a beginning of a map! There I learned about resilience and revisited and adapted the Wheel of Life.

Resilience is the ability to adapt and change when faced with new and often stressful circumstances. For me, it is about bouncing back and remaining hopeful. When you are resilient, you do more than just endure and persevere; you respond with active energy. You come through with exhilaration. You thrive!

According to Dr. Salvatore Maddi, psychologist and author of *Resilience at Work: How to Succeed No Matter What Life Throws at You*, there are three elements within resilience: challenge, commitment, and control. Dr. Maddi believes that if a person is strong in the element of challenge, they see stress and change as a learning experience. In the face of obstacles, a resilient person asks, "How can I learn from this? What does this have to teach me?"

The second element is commitment. Amidst the chaos of change, a resilient person pays attention to what is before him and tries to understand and interpret how it is affecting him. He remains committed to the process even when it's messy. It takes courage to remain on the journey when the destination is unclear. Committed individuals choose to stay involved rather than to become isolated.

The third element is control. The resilient person begins to develop a sense of hopefulness rather than lapse into passivity and powerlessness. He begins to think about how he can use this experience to help others.

The idea of resilience touched me profoundly. I am tremendously grateful for this learning experience. It led me to seek out the National Alliance on Mental Illness to start asking,

"How can I learn from this?" It has encouraged me to be aware of my choices and how they affect my health. And it has guided me into a more hopeful place, and to writing this book. I have learned that knowing who you are and showing up as your authentic self with all your imperfections can be a powerful witness to others. If we wait until we are perfect before we share our story, we waste precious time, hide our gifts, and miss out on the chance to help others. Stories have the power to change us and others. Sharing them reminds us of where we have been, helps us see where we are, and directs us toward unanticipated paths.

To be sure, telling our truth and working from the heart is hard. It is rarely ever comfortable. It feels risky, and makes me feel exposed. I also know that sharing my story is part of my continuing journey to be whole and healthy. It is my way of acknowledging my fears and ensuring my forward movement toward health. And it is about fulfilling my purpose. Dr. Brene Brown says, "If we want greater clarity in our purpose… vulnerability is the path." And so it goes.

Chapter 3:
Remember to Breathe

"Breathing in, I calm my body. Breathing out, I smile. Dwelling in the present moment, I know this is a wonderful moment." —Thich Nhat Hanh

Breathe in through your nose and out through your nose.

In 2, 3, 4, 5, 6, 7. Out 2, 3, 4, 5, 6, 7, 8, 9, 10, 11…

In 2, 3, 4, 5, 6, 7. Out 2, 3, 4, 5, 6, 7, 8, 9, 10, 11…

My coach, Lee, has us lying on the carpeted floor, eyes closed, arms comfortably at our sides with hands relaxed—or better yet, with hands on our bellies. With our hands on our bellies, we can feel them lift up and down as the air moves in and out. Breathe in, belly rises. Breathe out, belly goes down. For a few minutes, we breathe together.

Breathe in through your nose and out through your nose.

In 2, 3, 4, 5, 6, 7. Out 2, 3, 4, 5, 6, 7, 8, 9, 10, 11…

In 2, 3, 4, 5, 6, 7. Out 2, 3, 4, 5, 6, 7, 8, 9, 10, 11…

In that moment, hope grew as a yearning, the way leaves turn up to cup the moisture in the air before a rain. It was as if my body was nourished with a cool glass of water, and a freshness of hope permeated my body. It came gently though only after I was able to quiet my mind, stirring me like a holy breath. Perhaps it was my "inner coach" speaking to me. By slowing down and calming my mind, I started to think more clearly. I began to think there were opportunities to create a new way of being with my son, a healthier way for him and for myself. My invitation to hope came gently like ripples upon a pond.

I have come to understand that breath is a gateway to healing and transformation. When I was standing in the middle of what was broken, chaotic, and frightening, I felt like I was in a boat being tossed about by raging storm waves. Only when I was reminded to breathe, slow down, and calm my mind was I able to see the ripples on the surface of the pond as possible next right steps to take on my journey to healing myself and my relationship with my son. It was a small shift in my thinking, but it made all the difference in that moment.

Now I understand that every mind state is workable. I am able to recognize when I am feeling pain in my ribcage, shortness of breath, fuzziness in my thoughts, and doing a lot of sighing. When I am breathing shallowly, or maybe even holding my breath without knowing it, my "coach" is saying, "Just breathe." Shallow breathing means less oxygen in the bloodstream, increased muscle tension, and headaches. I have heard it said that we can go weeks without food, days without water, but only a few minutes without oxygen. That alone should tell us about the importance of conscious, mindful breathing to nourish our body one cell at a time.

Yoga, meditation, Tai Chi, and Qi Gong all stress the importance of correct breathing. There are many helpful resources available to learn these practices. The 7-11 breathing technique taught by my coach requires no costly equipment or resources. You can do this anywhere. You can sit in class, at your desk at work, even in an airport, and close your eyes. Taking deep belly breaths sends an all-clear signal to your nervous system that triggers a relaxation response. The reason for the longer, slower release of the breath through your nose is to give the relaxation response more time to kick in. Your heart will beat more slowly, your blood pressure will lower, and your muscles will unwind and release tension.

On the out breath, you might want to smile gently. Smiling relaxes hundreds of muscles in the face. Etty Hillesum said, "Sometimes the most important thing in a whole day is the rest we take between two deep breaths." So, are you ready?

Breathe in through your nose and out through your nose.

In 2, 3, 4, 5, 6, 7. Out 2, 3, 4, 5, 6, 7, 8, 9, 10, 11…

In 2, 3, 4, 5, 6, 7. Out 2, 3, 4, 5, 6, 7, 8, 9, 10, 11…

Chapter 4:
Create Healing Space

"Where flowers bloom, so does hope."
—Lady Bird Johnson

How does a seed know when it is time to burst from its protective coating? Scientists have discovered the genetic "wiring" that helps a seed know the perfect time to germinate. When deciding whether to germinate or remain dormant, seeds in the soil sense cues in the environment such as temperature, light, moisture, and nutrients. After taking time to heal we also will take our cues from the environment that it is no longer healthy or desirable to stay in the dark. The right environment or healing space gently invites us to begin again. This often happens almost without perception. We realize one day that we have broken through and we are beginning to green, slowly and tenderly.

In my healing space, I have little pockets of hope everywhere on my bookshelves. Two birds huddle atop the word HOPE. It was waiting for me at Pier 1. It, along with a copy of Emily Dickinson's poem, remind me to keep hope alive.

Hope is the thing with feathers
that perches in the soul,
And sings the tune without the words
And never stops at all . . .

A print of Georgia O'Keefe's *Black Hollyhock Blue Larkspur,* 1930, along with a gold hanging star from a dear friend, prompt me to trust "the star in my heart," my inner wisdom. An acorn from the oak grove of my sons' university recalls my inner potential waiting to grow mightily. Of course, I also have many, many books on my bookshelves. I swear sometimes books have literally jumped off the shelf to get my attention! Books that have contributed to my resiliency include:

- *Walking Meditation* by Nguyen Anh-Huong & Thich Nhat Hanh

- *Daring Greatly* by Brene Brown, Ph.D., LMSW

- *Giving Thanks: The Gifts of Gratitude* by MJ Ryan

- *God's Hotel: A Doctor, A Hospital, and a Pilgrimage to the Heart of Medicine* by Victoria Sweet

- *The Star in My Heart: Experiencing Sophia, Inner Wisdom* by Joyce Rupp

- *A Life of Being, Having, and Doing Enough* by Wayne Muller

Glimpses of hope like these kept appearing from every-where. They sustained me and gave me nourishment for the journey. I welcomed them like those leaves turning up to cup the moisture in the air before the rain.

Other healing spaces for me included being out on my deck or wandering in the woods. In the spring, I would eagerly search for signs of new life. I would gently move aside the dead leaves to see if the crocuses were coming up, and carefully cover them back up so as to not disturb their natural cues to start greening. I was trying to uncover my hope. My heart would be warmed by the appearance of the white flowers of the Hepatica, or buds on the Flowering Almond—which, incidentally, represent awakening and hope! Sometimes I would sit on my deck soak-ing up the sun. Listening to the birds singing in the trees and the small brook behind our house babbling was balm for my soul.

In my home, I have created a healing space with comfortable leather chairs with a prayer shawl to wrap around my shoulders. The chairs surround the bookshelf that displays the images and books that serve as touchstones to assure me that my life matters and encourage me to trust the journey. Because spending time in nature is healing energy, I try to bring nature inside with plants and a water fountain. I have small votive candles, my prayer box, and engraved inspiration stones. Also in my healing space I have a meditation shell, a symbol of new life that I hold in my hand as I journey through my meditations, and a hand-held labyrinth. Here I often have a cup of herbal tea, read, pray, and reflect.

I describe my healing spaces as examples; your healing spaces will look different. It will have things that are meaningful to you, that speak to your heart and your experiences. People who have visited my home often say, "If I lived here, I would never leave." I tell them, "You should create a healing space in your home. Everyone deserves one!"

When I attended ACI Coaching Skills Training at the Chautauqua Institute, I was struck by the image of a long bridge on the premises. I took a photograph of the bridge, strewn with fallen leaves. It looked like an invitation to somewhere I did not yet know. I paired the image with a song that I found by a young, then eight-year-old girl named Anna Graceman. Her musical piece was, "Take Me Where I Want to Go." I knew I wanted to feel whole again. I did not know that I would begin to see my chaotic experience as a gift. I did not know that on my healing journey I would be coached into my life's purpose. As Douglas Adams said, "I may not have gone where I intended to go, but I think I have ended up where I intended to be." I never dreamed I would write a book to help parents, students, or anyone who wants to model resilience in the face of whatever life throws at them. I never thought I would offer workshops on creative ways to mitigate stress. Interestingly enough, here I am.

Hope believes in the part of me that envisions me resilient and thriving. Hope is trusting that what has happened will someday make sense, or at least some good will come from it. I have come to trust the gardening process, and expect that my gifts and talents will blossom. I am determined to share the fragrance of hope and arrange my bouquet in such a way as to help others become their best, resilient selves.

Chapter 5:
Nourish Yourself

"To eat is a necessity, but to eat intelligently is an art."
—Francois de La Rochefoucauld

We can't be prepared for everything, for every stressor that will come our way. We can make intelligent choices about how we nourish ourselves. A wise choice can even provide quick relief for times when you need an immediate calming effect.

While I was writing this book, I was feeling like I had come to a roadblock in my creative process, and I was stressed. In fact, the funny thing was, I was writing this chapter about nourishing yourself, about the link between diet and stress, and boy was I feeling it! A fellow IIN student coached me. She advised, "Light a candle, take some time to meditate, have a cup of tea, and write from your heart." I did just that. In my healing space, I lit a beeswax candle; had a cup of jasmine, rose, mint, and goji berry tea (known to improve blood, nourish the body, promote circulation, and ease stress); and listened attentively while holding my lavender-stuffed heart from IIN. When I felt ready, I read some scripture for the day, which serendipitously included some thoughts on not knowing the "ins" and "outs" of the job and asking for a listening heart so one can lead well. The readings also had something to say about cultivating thankfulness. When I picked up a book, *Giving Thanks: The Gifts of Gratitude* by MJ Ryan, I flipped randomly to a page and read:

> *A perennial dieting tip is to eat something and then wait twenty minutes before deciding to eat something again. The reason is that your body needs that much time to register that it is full. If you keep eating without pausing, you will not realize that your body is full, and therefore you may overeat.*

> *Giving thanks for what we have in our lives is like that pause when eating. It allows us to feel full, to register on the emotional and spiritual level that we have, in fact, been given 'enough.' If we don't practice gratitude on a daily basis, it's easy...to feel a lack...on a psychological level we haven't registered that we already have what we need.*

Wow! Thank you for the wisdom to pause and nourish myself, to remind myself that I have what I need to accomplish this task.

No doubt the numerous sensory inputs of warm herbal tea, flickering candlelight, and fragrant lavender served to calm my central nervous system. As an Occupational Therapist, I have helped many students explore sensory input, and aided them in equipping their "toolbox" with sensory tools. These personal tools helped them to bounce back from overstimulation and focus on their job as student. You, too, can benefit from putting together a sensory "diet" that will help you in times of stress.

1. Put Something in Your Mouth
   - Drink warm tea.
   - Eat something chewy, like a bagel or string cheese.
   - Drink a smoothie through a straw.
   - Take slow, deep breaths.

2. Move
   - Do isometrics.
   - Rock in a chair.
   - Dance.
   - Jump on a mini trampoline.

3. Touch
   - Try holding and fidgeting with a Koosh ball, rubber bands, clay, scented bean bag.
   - Take a warm shower.
   - Pet or play with an animal.
   - Rub gently or vigorously on your skin.
   - Hold or lean against a large pillow.

4. Look
   - Dim lights, light a candle, watch the fire in the fireplace.
   - Watch fish in an aquarium.
   - Watch waves on the lake/ocean or wind in the

trees/tall grass.
- Gaze at a glitter wand or kaleidoscope.

5. Listen
    - Listen to classical type music (even, slow beat) or any music that is calming to you.
    - Listen to a water fountain or waves on the shore.
    - Listen to birds singing in the trees.

Experiment with different sensory input, and be aware of how it makes you feel. Listen to the inner wisdom of your body. Artfully put together your sensory tools. When you need them, pause and nourish your central nervous system. Your personal sensory diet will help you manage your stress.

The changes you make don't have to be monumental. The tiniest gestures can have a huge impact. Make sure you drink enough water. I bought myself a new glass water bottle with a colorful silicone sleeve. It was a small gesture and a minor shift, but it made all the difference for me. I now feel I am keeping myself much better hydrated with fewer headaches and more clarity.

Choose whole foods, those closest to nature. Processed foods contain excess sugar, salt, additives, and preservatives that only serve to stress your body more. A good rule of thumb is to read the label; if it has more than five ingredients and/or has contents that you cannot pronounce, it probably won't nourish you well. Eat regular and adequate well-balanced meals that contain protein, fruits and vegetables, dairy (if you tolerate it), nuts, seeds, and small amounts of grain.

Here you will have to experiment and listen to the wisdom of your body. Everybody is different. The important thing is to not skip and not skimp. Your body under stress is being depleted of important nutrients like vitamin B12, iodine, magnesium, vitamin D, calcium, folate, vitamin A, omega-3s, vitamin E, and iron. Your body needs to be consistently replenished so you have energy and can think clearly.

Help keep stress under control by eating a stress-busting food every day. Here are some stress-fighters with which I have been experimenting:

- **Kale**: Kale is a nutrient-dense food with an amazing amount of vitamins, minerals, and phytonutrients. It contains vitamin K, which helps in the production of anxiety-regulating neurotransmitters. Kale is also a good source of calcium, which helps in the relaxation of muscles. I have found it easy to incorporate chopped kale into soups, casseroles, and omelets for added stress-busting effects.

- **Better Meat**: Try crowding out processed meats like hot dogs, pepperoni, and deli meat in favor of wild-caught seafood and fish and organic, grass-fed sources of beef, pork, lamb, and chicken. Your body under stress needs to replenish protein, iron, and vitamin B12. These nutrients help your body produce serotonin, dopamine, and other mood-regulating neurotransmitters. Meat that is wild-caught, grass-fed, or pasture-raised ensures that it is more nutrient dense and contains more healthful antioxidants and omega-3s. There are vegetarian sources of protein as well. Again, experiment and find out what works best for you.

- **Farm-fresh eggs**: Eggs contain healthful amounts of folate, vitamin B12, choline, and vitamin D, all of which impact stress on your body. My family enjoys getting real pasture-raised eggs from our Mennonite neighbors. You can see the difference in nutrients right away in the dark orange yolks packed with more omega-3 fats and carotenoids.

- **Green Tea**: Green tea contains powerful anti-oxidants such as polyphenols, flavonoids, and catechins. These all serve to have a calming effect on the mind and body. I have learned to enjoy drinking 3-5 cups of yerba mate a day. Yerba mate is a South American beverage, and is made by steeping the leaves and stems of the yerba mate plant. It has 90% more antioxidants than regular green tea. I have found that it boosts my immune system, and improves my mental clarity, focus, and energy without giving me the "jitters" of caffeine. In fact, my husband, who has caffeine intolerance, is able to drink yerba mate without side effects. I am grateful that my youngest son introduced me to yerba after his trip to Uruguay.

- **Blueberries**: Blueberries contain plenty of antioxidants that help reduce stress levels. They also contain vitamins C and E, along with minerals like magnesium and manganese, which also help to mitigate stress. I enjoy our blueberries fresh-picked and frozen from our local organic blueberry patch. We love to put them in yogurt, smoothies, steel-cut oats, and salads.

- **Kefir**: Kefir is made by fermenting milk with kefir grains that are similar to tiny clumps of cauliflowers, wheat grain size or bigger, that no other milk product forms. Kefir is rich in vitamins A, B1, B12, D and K, biotin, and tryptophan—an essential amino acid that our body uses to produce serotonin, which promotes relaxing effects on our brain. Kefir has a relaxing effect on the nervous system, and may relieve symptoms of anxiety and benefit people who have sleeping problems. It also has positive effects on depression. Minerals contained in kefir, such as calcium, magnesium, and phosphorus, will additionally aid in keeping our nervous system healthy and functioning well. You can purchase kefir grains, or get them from someone who is already making kefir. I make small amounts every other day by leaving it out on my counter. When the kefir is ready, I like to add a banana and some blueberries in the blender.

- **Avocados**: Avocados are an excellent source of minerals, protein, and vitamins C and E. They also provide potassium and healthy fat, which are beneficial in regulating stress hormones by keeping your nerves and brain cells healthy. Avocados were new to me, and I have enjoyed experimenting by putting them in smoothies and salads. I even made a great chocolate "pudding" with avocado, banana, yogurt, a little milk and maple syrup Yum!

As you can see, it doesn't have to be complicated. The gestures can be small, but powerful. What wise choice will you make to change how you eat? What new tool will you put in your "sensory diet" toolbox? What new stress-buster food will you try?

Chapter 6
Connect with Others

"I define connection as the energy that exists between people when they feel seen, heard, and valued; when they can give and receive without judgment; and when they derive sustenance and strength from the relationship."—Brene Brown

NAMI (National Alliance on Mental Illness) is a non-profit, grassroots, self-help support and advocacy organization with more than 220,000 individual members working through more than 1,000 local and state affiliates. I was blessed to find a local NAMI chapter that offered a 12 week Family-to-Family class and a support group. There I discovered a place to be seen and heard. There I found a safe place to pour out my heart with people that "got it." I heard their stories, I made connections, and I started to get oriented for a bewildering and scary journey.

I discovered other professionals along the way who were willing to go the extra mile to support me, like the Social Worker at the hospital where my son was admitted. Through NAMI I was able to connect with the Family-to-Family instructor in the community where my son lived. I read books like *Hurry Down Sunshine* by Michael Greenburg, *Crazy: A Father's Search Through America's Mental Health Madness* by Pete Early, and *Where are the Cocoa Puffs?* by Karen Winters Schwartz. I am grateful to have had the opportunity to hear and meet both Pete Early and Karen Winters Schwartz when NAMI sponsored author talks at neighboring libraries and colleges.

I just needed to know that I was not alone on this journey. I wrestled with understanding brain biochemistry in a way I hadn't during my Occupational Therapy education. This was personal. I was receiving an extensive, dedicated education about mental illness. NAMI provided me with resources so I could learn as much as possible about brain disorders. Knowledge is strength. It served to provide a sense of relief, to know that I could do something. It lightened the load and gave me stamina to keep on walking.

Throughout the learning process, my instructors were vigilant guilt-busters. On more than one occasion I heard, "You can't know what no one ever told you." I was encouraged to always be attentive to my self-care. Their teachings slowly had an effect on me, and I began to realize that I had stopped blaming myself, or looking for someone else to blame for this new, unfair reality. I began to express my grief in healthy ways and help myself through the ups and downs, the periods of hope and disappointment.

I started wanting to educate others around me about mental illness. When I was invited to preach in my church in the absence of our pastor, I took the opportunity to connect the scripture and liturgy to the subject of mental illness and to personally tell my story. Thomas Horn said, "Grief, no matter where it comes from, can only be resolved by connecting to other people." I have found this to be true on my journey. I also sought out materials through my denomination to lead a series of conversations to increase awareness of mental illness and help congregations understand how they can compassionately respond. Those that joined me were individuals struggling with mental illness themselves, or within their families. I like to think we became beacons of hope in the darkness for one another. I began to trust my inner "coach" in showing me the way.

During the process, I learned to ask questions like, "What's useful here?" instead of "What did I do wrong?" I was guided by wondering, "What can I learn from this? What's the solution to that?" I learned that each of us is on a courageous journey and has something of value to share with others. And others have something of value to teach us. I was becoming more and more resilient.

Feeling seen, heard, and valued is what I experienced in my coaching for transformation team. To be sure, it was a challenge for me, a place of vulnerability. It turned out to be a safe place to be vulnerable, and a route to greater clarity. We were learning as a team to trust one another as we learned new skills together.

Our gifts were artfully coming together to be of service for transformation within our congregations and our denomination.

Being valued for the gifts I brought to the team encouraged me to continue even when the way seemed unclear. It seems that receiving and appreciating kindness, receiving and giving hope, are powerful gestures. And gratitude turns out to be an important part of resiliency. In the midst of adversity, gratitude for the things that are going right helps put things into perspective.

During our coaching skills training, we were invited to help our congregations create "river stories" rather than "rut stories." We learned that river stories energize and carry us toward possibility of purpose, while rut stories focus on scarcity and negativity, and keep us mired in the past. In the river stories, I was invited to remember my potential and discover my purpose. My inner coach came along side me to clarify and encourage me to take the next right steps in this coaching journey. I was given support from fellow team members to develop new skills; I was being fed, growing and expanding my possibilities.

I felt a deep sense of commitment to the coaching team, and eventually a desire to stay committed to the process of becoming a coach and a member of the coaching team. I share this experience with you so you know this is not always a straightforward process. On the first night of training, I felt completely overwhelmed. I could feel myself disengaging, and seriously beginning to doubt my abilities and even my reason for being at the training. Exhausted, I went to sleep that night thinking that I had made a mistake and I was not going to be able to keep up my responsibility to the team. Somehow, during the night, my inner coach worked with me. When I awoke the next morning, I was convinced that I was going to be a part of the team. I had a plan to develop the skills I needed. I still felt fearful, but energized at the same time. I was determined to feel the fear and do it anyway! I was building resilience and working on the habit of moving toward discomfort instead of running away from it.

What struck me then, and still causes me to pause and ponder, is how this challenge has mirrored the challenge in my personal life. Each has informed the other. And I continue to discover that true vulnerability is the path to clarity in our purpose. I am grateful for my connections that lift me up and accompany me on this journey.

According to Paul Pearsall in *The Heart's Code: Tapping the Wisdom and Power of Our Hearts*, "There is no more obvious evidence of connection between our heart and energy outside the body than our heart's response to musical rhythms… and health happens when we are in rhythm within ourselves, synchronized with other living systems and moving to our preset beat rather than trying to respond to the driving beat of the stressful outside world…Healing, then, becomes the ability of our heart to improvise and develop its own new rhythms to the chaotic rhythms that continually emerge in our daily life."

I was trying to reconnect with something that had been missing; trying to re-member my reassuring inner rhythms that had been disrupted. This is what I was desperately seeking, and what I gratefully found, when I discovered drumming for health and drumming circles.

A young woman sits in a circle of chairs in the basement of a church playing her djembe, a West African healing drum. Gradually, others arrive, carrying various hand drums. My husband, friend, and I join them, and are invited to pick a drum that "speaks" to us. We join the circle and begin playing our own personal rhythms on our drums. It isn't long before our individual rhythms find a common pulse. My shoulders relax, my breathing becomes deeper, and my mind grows calm and centered in the moment. On the facilitator's cue, we all end together: 1-2-3-BOOM. Rest.

This natural coming together of the various personal rhythms into one harmonious drum song was and is amazing. Somehow, drumming in community helps us turn off the overthinking parts of our brains and allows us to deeply listen to ourselves and others. When we begin to express our deep emotions and pay attention to others through the drumming process, we organically move to unity. It's not at all about judging performance; it's about creating something together.

I experience drumming as medicine for the heart. Drum circles are a safe and sacred space. It is a space where healing can happen, where we can let go of emotions, and where we can share hope without speaking a word.

Your search for knowledge and support will lead you on different paths. Your level of "just right" stress to keep you moving forward will be particular to you. The tools you choose and the community you connect with will reflect your authentic self. To be sure, genuine connecting is often uncomfortable. You will have to take some risks and learn to trust yourself and your inner coach. Allowing oneself to be vulnerable and learning to trust are part of becoming resilient.

I offer this invitation from Christine Stevens: "to let go of whatever it is you would like to release today. Visualize or even speak one thing you would like to release in the now. Using your voice, vocalize the release with 'Ahhhh,' a deep sigh or any sound you choose. Brush your drum away from your body, in a gesture of sweeping away anything you no longer need. Tap – Tap – Tap, Ahhhh (Brush). Tap – Tap – Tap, Ahhhh. Tap – Tap – Tap, Ahhhh. Tap – Tap – Tap, Ahhhh. As you complete this rhythm…rest, feeling the renewal and peace."

Chapter 7
Keep Walking

"It is solved by walking."—St. Augustine

Well, maybe I haven't been able to solve it. But through all the stress and grieving, I have been able to continue to move forward. Labyrinth and Tai Chi walking have been tools and strong symbols for me as I "keep on walking" this often difficult path.

In the confusing early days of discovering my son's illness, as I returned from a long walk, I noticed a thistle growing up out of the gravel in our driveway. It caught my attention, the beauty of that flower. I thought, "Even amongst the most prickly, hurtful situations, good can come." Nothing had changed about my son's situation, and yet that shift in my perspective had changed everything for me in that moment. John Muir says,

"...in every walk with Nature one receives far more than he seeks." I have learned that the thistle is a symbol for persistence. It is able to survive—even thrive—when others cannot in harsh conditions. That perchance walk gifted me with a very powerful image that continues to inspire me with hope. It reminds me of my unfolding resilience whenever I need it.

There is a legend about the thistle protecting the Scots. It is said that when an invading Viking army was trying to sneak up at night on a Scots encampment, a barefoot enemy stepped on a thistle, which caused him to cry out in pain and alert the Scots. In gratitude, the plant became known as the Guardian Thistle. I carry my Guardian Thistle image close to my heart as I keep walking this journey. What image of resilience speaks to your heart? Seek it and keep it close for whenever you need it.

Another powerful symbol of life's journey is the labyrinth. A labyrinth is a single, circular path that leads, reliably, into the center and back out again. The path is not a puzzle to be solved or a maze with choices to be made. There are no wrong turns in a labyrinth. Walking the geometric pattern of the path is a journey that is used as a tool for reflection, discernment, transformation, healing, and wholeness.

There is a long history of labyrinths being used, and many can be found on hospital and school campuses, at churches, or in private gardens. Walking a labyrinth is "highly effective for reducing anxiety and producing what's called the relaxation response," says Dr. Herbert Benson, a professor of medicine at Harvard Medical School. It can lower blood pressure and breathing rates, and improve focus and clarity of thoughts. Labyrinth walking can also help with conflict resolution, grief, and depression. At its heart, the labyrinth offers time and space for people to be more reflective and quiet. It is a place where transformation and healing can happen.

One day when I was feeling particularly stretched thin emotionally and physically, I felt the tug of the labyrinth on my heart. I drove to a nearby town to walk the path with which I was familiar. But this day, I was urged to take off my shoes and walk the path barefooted. Not far into the journey, I was thinking, "Why did I do this? This is painful!" Slowly I began to notice that I was walking differently. I was placing my feet carefully, shifting my weight to adjust to the stones beneath my feet. I realized that it was not unlike how I was learning to adjust my life's walk with my son, to respond in a healthier way. Adjustments had to be made to mitigate the pain. Again, a little shift in perception made a huge impact on my ability to keep moving forward on this journey.

I have learned that walking the labyrinth is not really about the destination; it's about the process, the journey itself. Labyrinths are a metaphor for the journey to the center of your deepest self and back out into the world with an expanded understanding of who you are. Your journey is particular to you. It is about change, moving forward, expanding your vision of possibilities, learning to see clearly and deeply, listening to your inner coach, and taking courageous steps. I hope that each of you has the opportunity to experience the healing potential of a labyrinth. To find a labyrinth near you, visit www.labyrinthsociety.org.

Another form of walking that has been beneficial to me is Tai Chi walking. Research has shown that regular Tai Chi practice reduces stress, anxiety, and depression, along with a host of other health benefits. Noticing our breath and focusing on slow, mindful movements leaves less room for our minds to jump from one subject to another, losing its focus and going down the path of fear and negativity. Tai Chi walking, moving meditation, brings our mind back to our breath, to the here and now.

It doesn't have to be complicated. A small gesture of mindful, slow walking of any kind can have the same benefits. Thich Nhat Hanh describes walking meditation as taking slow, mindful steps with a smile on your face. Smiling in gratitude to whatever you are aware of in the moment is an important part of the practice. You might smile in gratitude to your breath, to the birds that sing, to a thistle growing in the gravel—whatever you notice. He suggests measuring your number of steps by the rhythm of your breaths. Breathe in, one, two, three. Breathe out, one, two, three. In this way, the stepping and the breath become one. He says, "When [you] practice walking meditation, [you] do not try to arrive anywhere or attain any particular goal. [Your] destination is the here and now."

This is a practice that costs nothing and can be done anywhere, inside or outside. When walking indoors, the teacher recommends "that you take off your shoes. You can feel the floor and connect with the Earth more easily without shoes.

The flow between you and Mother Earth then becomes stronger." I have found this to be true in my practice. I like to think of my roots going deep, deep into the earth, leaving me feeling centered and grounded. I also find it helpful to add a breath prayer. On the in breath I think, "In this moment…" On the out breath I think, "Let it go." Find your own words that have meaning for you and help you feel calm and settled. The longer you practice walking with this connection, the deeper the transformation. You might eventually be able to smile in your stressful situation or pain and see it as a gift. You might quiet the mind enough to hear your inner coach whispering to you, "Keep on walking. Walking is life. You are still alive; the journey is not done."

If you would like to learn more, *Walking Meditation* by Nguyen Anh-Huong & Thich Nhat Hanh is a wonderful resource and includes an instructional DVD and five guided meditations on CD.s

Chapter 8
Build Your Resilience Circle

"I pin my hopes to quiet processes and small circles, in which vital and transforming events take place."—Rufus Jones

Circles continue to show up and echo throughout my journey to resilience. From the labyrinth's spirals, drumming circle gatherings, the Wheel of Life tool, to creating my various circles of support—indeed, to the very journey of life itself— there it is, in all its constancy! Circles provide me with spiritual sustenance and speak to something deep in my spirit. I keep that image close to my heart, and somehow feel more secure in that image.

Circles and hoops are symbols in many ancient traditions. They have been revealed in petroglyphs, artifacts, words, and pictures carved in stone that date back thousands of years.

Sacred hoops appear in the medicine wheel, stone structures constructed by certain indigenous peoples of North America for various healing and teaching purposes. How fitting that the image becomes consequently conspicuous for me as I write about creating my resilience circle that includes chiropractic care, acupuncture, and massage therapy.

According to Dr. Mike Vorozilchak, "chiropractic care is one of the most powerful ways to overcome the defense physiology caused by chronic stress because of the impact it has on the brain and nervous system. When you receive care over time, you broaden your range of adaptability so that you are more equipped to handle stress, thereby minimizing its negative impact and maximizing your health and function."

He points out, "Negative/destructive stressors cause our body to go into 'defense mode' and alter our body's tension, tone, movement, and alignment. These intelligent and adaptive changes help us survive the moment but, what happens when they are kept up for days, weeks, months, and years?" He invites us to "look around and see it everywhere! We get sick. We lose energy. We develop health problems. Our body breaks down. We suffer needlessly…"

Dr. Mike believes, "that is where chiropractic care becomes an essential part in maximizing your health and well-being. Spinal adjustments help 'break the cycle' and help release tension and restore alignment and mobility. When this happens, a person is 'clear' and the cycles of communication between the brain and body resume at 100%. Over time, this allows the body to heal and repair itself and maintain a higher level of resistance to the stressors it faces."

I came to Dr. Mike hoping to mitigate the stress in my life, and to boost my immune system. I have gained so much more in the process. I have noticed more clarity of thought, increased energy, deeper sleep, and a general increased sense of well-being. On particular days in the process of writing this book, I have gratefully experienced a sense of breaking through a writer's block. Following treatment on what I have dubbed as my "wellness Wednesdays," I have felt the creative juices flowing much more freely. My decision to seek chiropractic care has proven to be a wise choice and a valuable support in building my resilience.

Equally important in my resilience circle is acupuncture. According to Ann Cain Crusade, RN, MSAOM, "Acupuncture is 'tailor-made' for assisting in the management of stress; it has a profound effect on our being." She likens it to "replenishing that deep internal well that we draw upon daily in order to cope emotionally, physically, and spiritually." Studies have shown that the elevated cortisol levels promoted by excessive stress are modulated with acupuncture treatment. At the same time, acupuncture has been proven to elevate the 'feel good' neurotransmitters produced in our brains. Ann notes that "post-treatment, people often enjoy that sense of deep relaxation or the acupuncture high."

Western scientific studies are only confirming what has been long known in acupuncture circles: Acupuncture works on a profoundly deep level. It can positively affect our chemistry and our ability to cope with stress, relieve depression, support memory and concentration, calm the heart and mind, ease anxiety and worry, support digestion and circulation, and promote deeper sleep. Even for those without a more serious condition, acupuncture can support well-being. Ann calls this a "tune-up."

Imagine you are lying on your back, your head, neck, and knees gently cradled. Your eyes remain softly closed while the pleasant weight of an eye pillow provides soothing, light pressure around your eyes. You are safe and cared for. You hear birds and the gentle sound of water in the distance. You are very still and you have nowhere to go, nothing to do. You just are. You feel a profound sense of peace, and all your tension melts away as the first needle is put in place. This is the kind of relaxation I have experienced through acupuncture.

I explored acupuncture as way to boost my immune system, and have remained healthy in the midst of tremendous stress. Beyond finding relaxation, I have found treatment to promote vibrant energy, deeper sleep, and clarity of thought. It has provided me with quiet space where true transformation and shifts of perspective have happened. I welcome and truly value this quiet process into my resilience circle.

In my search for any and all experiences that would be healing and stress-busting, I decided to try Massage Therapy to help build my resiliency in the face of so much stress. Much of the time I was in constant stress mode; sometimes because of specific crises, other times just as a result of ruminating on the past or thinking anxiously of what the future might hold. I have learned how important it is to be in the present, dealing with one day at a time and finding joy in the present moment. You can't change the past, and you can't change another person; you can only change how you respond. You can learn to promote your own health, to build your resilience.

Joy Perry, LMT, sees her role as taking you out of the fight or flight environment. When you attend a session with her, she is totally focused on you emotionally, physically, and spiritually. Joy says, "When I can take someone who is operating from the sympathetic state and move them to the parasympathetic state where they can enter rest and repair, I feel accomplished." According to Perry, "Massage Therapy enhances the immune system by stimulating lymph flow, relieves depression, pumps oxygen and nutrients into tissues and vital organs and improves circulation." In addition, she notes, "In the process endorphins, the 'feel good' hormone as well as serotonin, dopamine and oxytocin are released." Studies have also shown that cortisol levels also drop resulting in a relaxation response.

Joy's intention of "taking you out of the 'fight/flight' environment" is evident from the moment you enter her Barrington Holistic Spa. You are welcomed and invited to sit comfortably and have a bottle of water as she listens deeply to you explain your health history and your expectations for your session. Upon entering the therapy room, which is dimly lit, you are treated to a warmly flickering fireplace; gentle, soothing music; and a therapy table covered with heated flannel sheets.

You may choose from a variety of fragrant essential oils to be mixed with a carrier oil for your massage. Think "sensory diet." Think of this as space and time where healing can take place. It is time and space to slow down, to bring to mind all that is good in your life, rather than concentrating on the not so good. It is your "tincture of time."

As I look back, I was motivated to choose alternative medicine modalities because they matched my belief in treating the whole person: mind, body, and spirit. I also resonate with the underlying trust in the body's innate healing ability when given what it needs. I wanted to let go of the notion that I was powerless on this unexpected, painful journey that I found myself on. I wanted to let go of the notion that my life now was one of anxiety and worry about the future, so much so that I would miss the joys of the present. I believe that you and I can learn to promote our own health and resiliency. I share with you my experience of creating a supportive, healing resilience circle as an example. You will build a circle of resilience that works for you. Explore and build it!

Chapter 9
Find Your Voice

"When you give yourself permission to communicate what matters to you in every situation you will have peace despite rejection or disapproval. Putting a voice to your soul helps you to let go of the negative energy of fear and regret."
—Shannon L. Alder

What matters to you? What is worth doing even if you fail? What brings tears to your eyes or a lump in your throat? What are you going to do about it? My decision to share my story and walk alongside others as they take steps on their own personal journeys to wholeness necessitates me reliving some painful memories and "putting a voice to [my] soul." I have to show up, to be heard and seen. Speaking my truth is risky, but I believe in the end will be a gift.

Brene Brown speaks of vulnerability, saying, "It's life asking, are you all in? Can you value your own vulnerability as much as you value it in others? [Answering yes to these questions is] courage beyond measure. It's daring greatly. And often the result of daring greatly isn't a victory march as much as it is a quiet sense of freedom mixed with a little battle fatigue." So as tired as I am, I hear my inner coach encouraging me, "You have a story to tell and a vision of how things can be different that needs to be heard." I know in my heart that it will serve to strengthen my spiritual, emotional, and occupational aspects of my whole self, and keep me moving forward on my healing journey. So here I go, one halting step at a time.

I received a call that my son was in the hospital and would be undergoing surgery that afternoon or evening. I hurried to the hospital, two hours away, to find my son in excruciating pain from a deep wound in his backside. The infection was spreading. I learned that he had walked two miles to the emergency room that morning. By evening, he was in surgery. The wound was enormous, deep, and scary. The surgeon compassionately said, "I don't know what's happened to your son. I'm sorry." Each morning, the surgeon came to check him and change his dressing by pulling the packed gauze from the wound, pouring antiseptic solution into the gaping sore, and repacking it. It was excruciatingly painful for my son, and heart wrenching as a parent. He received large doses of intravenous antibiotics and pain medication, and still the infection was not clearing up.

On the fourth day, the surgeon decided to send my son

to the Intensive Care Unit. I knew it was bad! He was literally fighting for his life. I was so overwhelmed that I could not bear to stay in the room this time and listen to my son groan and cry in pain. I headed down the hall toward the hospital chapel to pray for strength, courage, and healing. I have found that synchronicity—or, as I believe, the Spirit— always places you where you need to be. As I sat texting family and friends to please pray for my son, I overheard a conversation between the Hospitalist and the ICU doctor. They clearly and audibly named my son. The hospitalist said, "I don't know why [the surgeon] is sending him over here. He should just patch him up and send him home. He just needs to be a man." The words pierced my heart. I know I must have looked ashen when I joined my husband in the ICU waiting room; he knew immediately that something was wrong. I told him I had overheard a conversation in the hall that made me seriously worry that our son might not receive the care that he needed. We asked to speak with the ICU doctor immediately.

My husband told the ICU doctor that I had overheard a conversation in the hall about our son. At first he acted confused, like he did not know anything about the conversation. My husband turned to me and asked, "Is this one of the doctors you saw and heard talking about our son?" I answered, "Yes, yes it is." The doctor then apologetically said that the hospitalist simply did not understand why the surgeon was sending our son over to ICU. We voiced the expectation that our son would get the very best care regardless of his mental, emotional, or financial status. Believe me, it took every ounce of courage to stand up to the powers that be, the authority, the doctor in charge. In that moment, I had to think about what I wanted, not about what I feared.

As writer Saul Bellow notes, "There was a disturbance in my heart, a voice that spoke there and said, I want, I want, I want! It happened every afternoon, and when I tried to suppress it, it got even stronger." I wanted my son to receive the care he needed. I wanted him to be treated with dignity. I wanted no other parent to suffer the way I had, hearing that conversation. I have learned that nothing will change unless you speak the words you hold inside. There are positive, healthy ways to stand up for what is right. I decided to write a letter to the hospital board and chairman. I wrote it to commend one of the nurses on the third floor and to make them aware of the unfortunate situation that occurred while my son was a patient in their hospital.

I included in the package a copy of the book *God's Hotel: A Doctor, A Hospital, and a Pilgrimage to the Heart of Medicine* by Victoria Sweet that I had hoped they would pass on as a "thank you" gift to the nurse. I recommended that each and every one of the board members read and reflect upon this book. Kindness, respect, and compassion are what we experienced from this particular nurse at a most difficult time in our lives. She was willing to go the extra mile to help in the healing of our son. He was suffering from a horrific wound. She alone was willing to support him in the needed healing of a much deeper, spiritual wound—to see him as a whole person with mental health issues and personal environmental issues that would affect his healing. And for that I was truly grateful.

I shared with them that, unfortunately, kindness and respect were not what we experienced from all members of their staff. I communicated to them the conversation that I overheard and the heartbreak it caused me, to hear such disparaging remarks about my son. I wrote this not because I wanted to report something to be adjudicated, but so that this wouldn't happen to another parent. We suffer enough as a result of our son's mental health struggles. No parent should wonder whether their loved one will receive adequate, compassionate care—that it should depend on his mental and financial status. I never received a reply from the Chairman of the Board. Regardless, my spirit was strengthened by actively searching for my voice and clearing a path for it to emerge.

Even as I write this chapter, I know deep in my heart that there is something more for which I must stand up and find a voice. I know that I need to speak up about men as victims of domestic violence. I know that it will not be easily accepted. There is a cultural bias in our society regarding domestic violence for both men and women. Many find it hard to believe that a man can suffer abuse from a female partner, but it does happen. There are statistics available from the National Domestic Violence Hotline. I am not going to quote them, because I believe the statistics do not begin to give a clear, truthful picture. All cases of domestic violence are underreported, and statistics do not determine importance when it is your loved one who is at risk.

When your loved one has property like a cell phone destroyed, has craft tools displayed as weapons, suffers humiliation, is made to feel guilty, is isolated from family and friends, faces threats of losing his child, is prevented from getting and keeping a job, it is heartbreaking to see. To see your loved one have a moment of absolute lucidity about his situation, saying, "I have nothing left; she's taken everything from me," is haunting. To later have him say, "It's not always like that. She's a good person," is confounding. None of it makes sense! But all of it is true.

I know the statistics show that this scenario happens more often with women as the victim, but I'm telling you, it happens in reverse, too. Men don't report abuse for many of the same reasons women do not seek help. In addition, they face disparaging remarks like "He should just be a man." Whatever that means! I am disheartened that most literature is only presented in the voice of the female as victim and male as perpetrator. This is not helpful when you are trying to get your son, brother, or male friend to see that what he is experiencing is indeed abuse. Is it so hard to create and provide appropriately worded information? Can we not get to the point where we protect all vulnerable people—male, female, adult, or child— from emotional, physical, and sexual abuse? I will continue to seek clarity around what more I can do to give voice to this dilemma.

Finding my voice to speak about men as victims of domestic violence—indeed, to tell my whole story of seeking resilience in the face of great stress—is difficult. But I believe what Brene

Brown says: "The willingness to show up changes us. It makes us a little braver each time." I wish truth and vulnerability did not feel like a burden. I believe it is a pathway to spiritual and emotional strength and freedom.

Chapter 10
Be Grateful

"Beginning to tune into even the minutest feelings of…
gratitude softens us…If we begin to acknowledge these
moments and cherish them…then no matter how fleeting and
tiny this good heart may seem, it will gradually, at its own speed,
expand."—Pema Chodron

We have so much for which to be grateful! And that's a good thing, as it is apparently good for your health. According to M J Ryan in *Giving Thanks: The Gifts of Gratitude*, "Recent scientific research has begun to indicate that positive emotions, such as gratitude and love, strengthen and enhance the immune system, enabling the body to resist disease and recover more quickly from illness, through the release of endorphins into the bloodstream…Among other effects, [endorphins] stimulate dilation of the blood vessels, which leads to a relaxed heart." This gives new meaning to softening us.

I have experienced this softening, or relaxing of the heart, as I continue to nurture my capacity to be "in the moment." Slowing down, taking time to notice those images, lyrics, quotes, nature sightings, and ordinary conversations often creates an "aha moment." It illuminates simple truths and helps me make sense of my experience. I wish the same for you: that you take full inventory of your surroundings, always being aware and open to new information. This will enable you to shift your perspective and to recognize those opportunities for transformation. I believe the ability to be "in the moment" helps define what it means to be fully alive—thriving, not just merely surviving!

I am grateful for the developing capacity to trust myself and my inner coach. Even as I searched the many books I read for clues about how to survive the loss of the son I had known, I did not want to run from the experience, but hoped to learn from it and be transformed. I began trusting that I was exactly where I was meant to be. I learned that if I continue to journey toward the discomfort rather than run away from it, somehow I come out the other side more resilient. Writing this book has been an exercise in trust as I learn to find my voice and reveal my heart. I never imagined that one day I would see this whole experience as a gift. Today, I trust that it is all part of my healing journey. I know I am never really alone. Nurturing trust is a journey. There is no estimated time of arrival, no getting it right. It takes courage to learn to trust yourself and listen to your inner coach. Both have something to say to your listening heart. Please listen.

I remember saying to a friend, "I want more joy in my life." In *A Life of Being, Having and Doing Enough*, Wayne Muller says, "As we listen carefully for the next right thing, it is good for us to remember we are not necessarily seeking something we do not already have." I share the following two powerful stories with you that reveal this truth.

One of my son's former teachers shared with me how impressed he was with my son's demonstrated kindness and compassion for others. He said, "When other students struggle, your son is always willing to help." He mused that this was quite rare in young people of that age. It served to reconnect me with something that I love about my son. That teacher has long forgotten that brief conversation, but I have remembered it and cherished it. It was a small gesture and a tremendous gift.

After sharing my personal story in a message from the pulpit in my faith community, an elderly woman from the congregation was very gracious to me. Each week, Ruth was the one person who would lovingly inquire about how my son was doing. For the longest time, I did not realize she was calling me Joy. After some time had gone by, I uncomfortably realized she had been calling me by the wrong name. One day, when she asked me, "Joy, how is your son doing?" I said, "Ruth, my name isn't Joy. It's Dee." She said, "I know that. But whenever I see you smile, I see joy, so I call you Joy." Wow! Small gesture, big impact.

Wayne Muller says, "Make no mistake: Gratitude does not come swiftly or easily, nor does it in any way erase the searing grief of the loss, the pain or the fury of injustice. It merely invites something beautiful, fresh and new to grow and flourish right beside it." I am so grateful for Ruth's wisdom in helping me to see this.

I tell these two stories because they have helped me to realize something about grief and joy: They are more alike than what I would have ever thought. Each is an emotion that we feel deep in our souls, and both lead us down the path of gratitude. Grief reminds us of what matters most to us, and joy reminds us of the wonder and awe of life, especially when we've discovered how fragile it is. I am grateful for the messages my listening heart receives from those who are traveling this journey with me, even if unknowingly. I am encouraged by Wayne Muller's words: "How can we imagine that everything we have, everything given, each thing taken may, if our hearts become supple and tender enough to allow it in, become not only acceptable but a genuine, authentic blessing, however unexpected or unwanted, for which we cannot help but give thanks?"

I have heard it said that life will bring you pain all on its own; your responsibility is to create joy. I don't know about responsibility, but I believe it is a privilege to reveal the joy and release it in whatever small way I can into a world that sorely needs it. We need each other to help us see what was there all along.

In gratitude, I leave you with these lyrics from my friend david m. bailey:

"Let it go, let it feel. Let it go, let it heal. Let it go. There is nothing that your heart cannot survive. Let it go, you're alive."

Acknowledgements

I am grateful for the presence of the Spirit, my inner Coach who continues to show me the way and encourage me to take each new step on this journey.

Anne Waasdorp, I want to thank you from my heart for all that you have been to me and all that you have done for me. You have always supported me, prayed for me, and yes, even challenged me to be my best resilient self. I would not be where I am today as a Certified Health Coach or author without your care and friendship. I am truly grateful.

To Bethany Snyder, my editor, cover and book designer, thank you for holding my hand and sharing your expertise with me to bring this book to fruition. It means the world to me.

Jennyfer Gomez Aranda, you have encouraged me throughout the process of writing this book. Your advice, "light a candle, have a cup of tea, meditate, and write from your heart," got me through many challenging spots. It was just what I needed to persevere; you are such a blessing.

Ron Anderson, my husband and friend, thank you for patiently and wisely giving me space, time, and encouragement to share my heart in the pages of this book.

About the Author

When Dee realized her grown son had a serious mental illness, she discovered the importance of self-care.

In the midst of chaos and stress, she committed herself to a path of resilience and a rediscovery of gratitude and joy by seeking coaches and mentors. In the process, Dee started leading stress-relieving groups in labyrinth experiences and drumming up health circles.

From Occupational Therapist to Certified Holistic Health Coach and author, nurturing resilience and wholeness has been her passion.

One reader described her as "always working from her heart," while another declared her "a spirit filled, warm, compassionate and beautiful human being who listens you into feeling the freedom to be more yourself and when asked gives direct and helpful counsel."

When she is not playing with her furry companion, Hope, you can find her encouraging, writing, and speaking about connecting purpose and passion.

Meet Dee and stay in-the-know about upcoming offerings at www.resilientyoucoaching.com.

Resources

Brown, Brene, Daring Greatly: How the Courage to Be Vulnerable Transforms the Way We Live, Love, Parent, and Lead. New York: Gotham, 2012.

Cain, Susan. The Power of Introverts in a World That Can't Stop Talking. New York: Broadway Books, 2012.

Crusade, Ann Cain. Personal interview. 7 Dec. 2014.

Earley, Pete. Crazy: A Father's Search Through America's Mental Health Madness. New York: Berkley Books, 2006.

Greenberg, Michael. Hurry Down Sunshine. New York: Vintage Books, 2009.

Maddi, Salvatore R. and Deborah M. Khoshaba. Resilience at Work: How to Succeed No Matter What Life Throws at You. New York: AMACOM, 2005.

Muller, Wayne. A Life of Being, Having and Doing Enough. New York: Harmony Books, 2010.

Pearsall, Paul. The Heart's Code: Tapping the Wisdom and Power of Our Hearts. New York: Harmony Books, 1999.

Perry, Joy. Personal interview. 3 Feb. 2015.

Rankin, Lissa. "Meet Your Inner Pilot Light." Web log post. Owning Pink. N.p., n.d. Web.

Rupp, Joyce. The Star In My Heart: Experiencing Sophia, Inner Wisdom. Philadelphia: Innisfree Press, 1990.

Ryan, M. J. Giving Thanks: The Gifts of Gratitude. San Francisco, CA: Conari Press, 2007.

Schwartz, Karen Winters. Where Are the Cocoa Puffs?: A Family's Journey Through Bipolar Disorder. Norwood, NJ: Goodman Beck Publishing, 2010.

Stevens, Christine. The Healing Drum Kit. Boulder, CO: Sounds True, 2005.

Sweet, Victoria. God's Hotel: A Doctor, A Hospital, and a Pilgrimage to the Heart of Medicine. New York: Riverhead Books, 2012.

"Take Me Where I Want to Go." http://www.youtube.com/watch?v=-NOXm3m_E3M.

Thich Nhat Hanh and Anh-Huong Nguyen. Walking Meditation. Boulder, CO: Sounds True, 2006.

Vorozilchak, Mike. Personal interview. 13 Jan. 2015.

For more information on david m. bailey, visit www.davidmbailey.com.

National Alliance on Mental Illness (NAMI)
3803 N. Fairfax Drive, Suite 100
Arlington, VA 22203
Telephone: 703.524.7600
Website: www.nami.org

IIN is a trademark of Integrative Nutrition Inc.

CPSIA information can be obtained at www.ICGtesting.com
Printed in the USA
LVOW06s0721120715

445901LV00029B/567/P